# STEP-BY-STEP

# MAKING BOOKS

### CHARLOTTE STOWELL
### ILLUSTRATED BY JIM ROBINS

Kingfisher

KINGFISHER
An imprint of Larousse plc
Elsley House,
24-30 Great Titchfield Street,
London, W1P 7AD

First published by Kingfisher 1994

10 9 8 7 6 5 4 3 2 1

© Copyright Larousse plc 1994

A CIP catalogue record for this book is available from the British Library.

ISBN 1 85697 231 3

Edited by Deri Robins
Designed by Ben White
Illustrations by Jim Robins
Photographed by Rolf Cornell,
  SCL Photographic Services
Cover design by Terry Woodley
Typeset in 3B2 by
  Tracey McNerney
Phototypeset by SPAN
  (Southern Positives and Negatives),
  Lingfield, Surrey
Printed in Hong Kong

# CONTENTS

# WHAT YOU NEED

First of all, you'll need to collect together a basic book-maker's kit like the one shown in the photo. You'll also need a thick piece of card or hardboard, to protect your work surface from paint, cuts and scratches.

## Paper and Card

You'll need plenty of thick paper or thin card to make the pages, and some stiff card for hard covers.

Practise making books from scrap paper first. Then visit an art shop to see the huge range of beautiful paper and card that's available!

## Glue

PVA or children's glue is good for sticking paper and thin card together, and for making collages.

For more heavy-duty sticking (attaching a cover, for example), use safe household glues – *not* super glues.

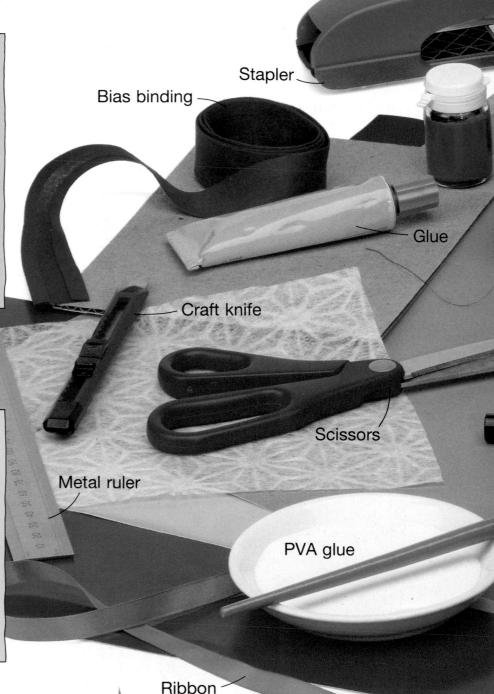

Stapler

Bias binding

Glue

Craft knife

Scissors

Metal ruler

PVA glue

Ribbon

## Tools of the Trade

To sew the pages of your books, you'll need a big darning needle, some strong thread and a pair of scissors. A stapler can also be used to make some simple books.

To cut the card and paper, you'll need to use a craft knife and a metal ruler. *Always* make sure an adult is around to watch and help when you're doing any cutting.

## Other Things

Among the other things you'll need are: poster paints, felt-tips and coloured pencils for colouring your books; strips of strong tape or bias binding for making hard covers; scraps of ribbon; some coloured fabric and paper; and a few large bulldog clips.

Poster paint

Strong thread

Paper and card

Bulldog clip

Felt-tips

Pencil

Cotton tape

Brushes

String

# MAKING BOOKS

The following pages show you how to make books of all shapes and sizes – just follow the step-by-step instructions carefully. Here are some tips on cutting and folding, along with some of the terms you'll meet throughout the book.

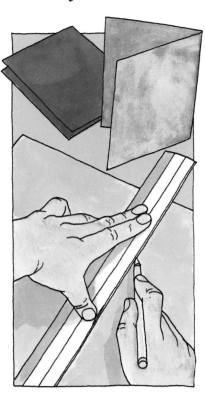

The *illustrations* are the pictures in your book.

A *spread* is two pages that face each other.

The *text* is all the words in the book.

The *heading* is usually bigger than the other words on the page.

## Folding

Folding card and thick paper is much easier if you run a used-up biro (or the back of your craft knife) lightly over the line first – this technique is called *scoring*.

*Endpapers* are stuck between the covers and the first and last pages of the book.

Spine

Front
cover

The *gutter* runs down
the middle of the spread.

Although the books
shown on the following
pages come in many
different shapes and
sizes, the basic parts are
the same. These parts
are all labelled here.

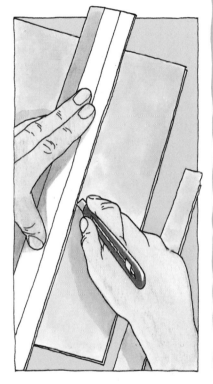

## Cutting

Craft knives are very
sharp, and need to be
handled with care!

Don't press too hard
– several light strokes
are best. A metal ruler
will help you to keep the
lines straight.

# FOLDERS & WALLETS

Folders and wallets have lots of different uses – unlike 'proper' books, you can change the contents as often as you like! You can also tuck in extra bits and pieces, such as maps, photos, magazine cuttings – even a booklet or two.

## Folder

Fold a big piece of fairly stiff card in half (see the notes on folding and scoring on page 6).

Cut another piece, slightly smaller than one half of the folder, and with flaps on two sides.

Cut several more pieces of card, each one smaller than the last. Fold the flaps, and glue them inside the folder as shown. Leave to dry.

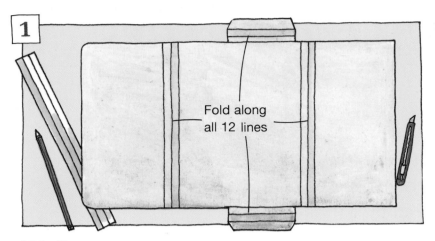

**1** Fold along all 12 lines

**2**

## Wallet

Take a pencil and a ruler, and copy the pattern shown above onto a sheet of thick paper or thin card.

Cut it out, using a ruler and a craft knife. Score along all the inside lines with an old biro, or the back of the craft knife.

Fold along the lines. Make the middle fold first, then fold in the opposite direction along the two other folds.

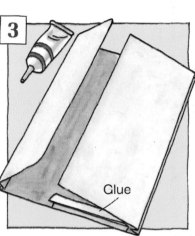

**3** Glue

To finish your wallet, glue the top of the side flaps inside the bottom fold, as shown.

*Left: A colourful selection of wallets and folders made from card.*

# SEWING THE PAGES

The following pages show three different ways of sewing the pages of your book.

If you want to add a cover (see pages 14-15) to the books shown in methods A and B, you must strengthen the spine with a strip of card. However, if you don't want to add a cover, you can leave this out.

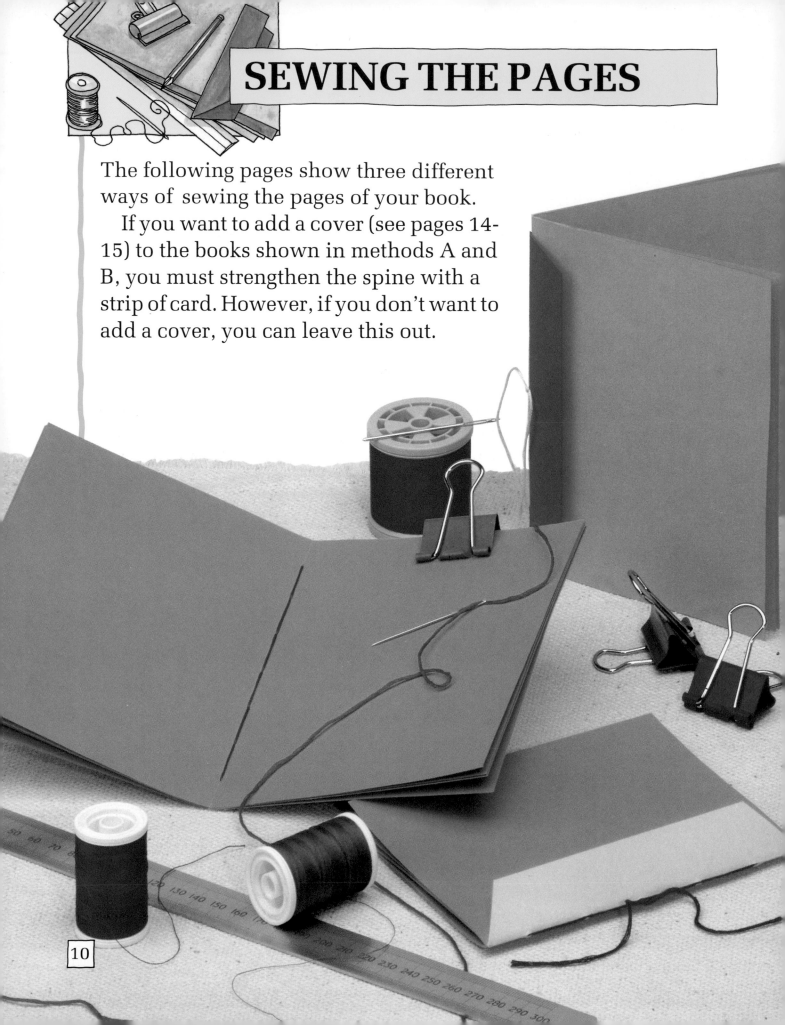

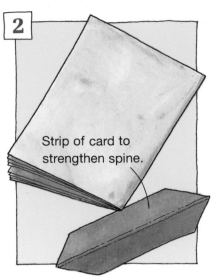

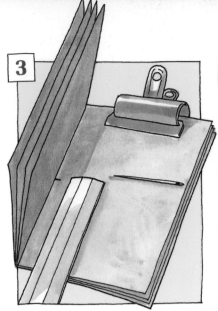

## Method A

Take up to six pieces of strong paper or thin card. Fold them down the middle, and stack them inside each other to make a book.

Cut a strip of card, the same length as your book. Trim the top and bottom diagonally, as shown, and fold around the spine of your book.

Hold the pages of your book tightly in place with a bulldog clip. Then take a ruler and pencil, and mark the middle point along the gutter.

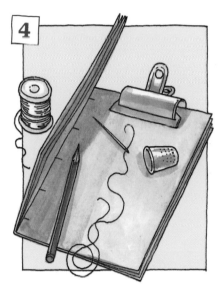

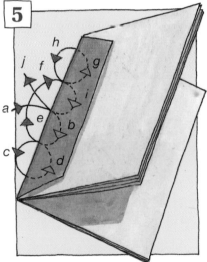

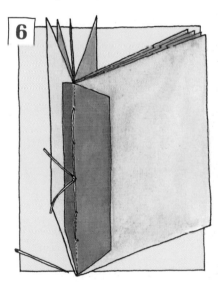

Strip of card to strengthen spine.

Add two more marks on each side of the middle mark, making them the same distance apart. Push a darning needle through all the pencilled marks.

Push the needle and thread through the middle mark, starting from the outside. Keep sewing in and out, following the direction shown above.

You should end up with two loose ends of thread outside the spine, as here. Tie them together with a double knot in the middle, and trim the ends with scissors.

## Method B

Fold a big piece of paper in half several times (two folds make an 8-page book, three folds make a 16-page book, and four folds make 32 pages). Add a strip of card along the spine, as shown in step 2 of method A (see page 11).

Sew exactly as shown for method A. Take a ruler and craft knife, and neatly trim all the edges except the spine.

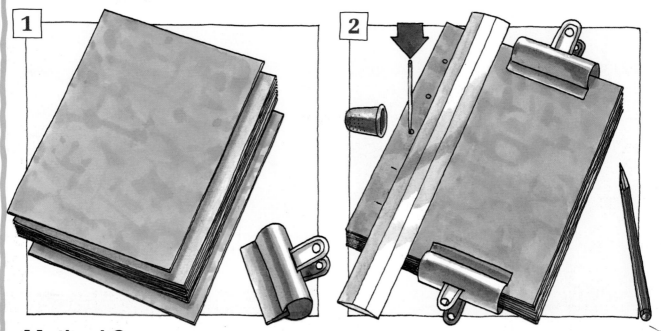

## Method C

Take several sheets of paper of the same size, and stack them in a pile. Cut two card covers, and place them at the top and bottom of the pile. Hold everything in place with bulldog clips.

Take a ruler and pencil, and draw a line 6 mm in from the spine. Mark five points along the line, all the same distance apart, and pierce them with a darning needle.

**3**

Thread the needle with strong thread. Sew around the spine in the direction shown in the picture.

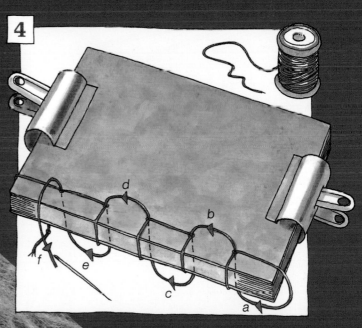

**4**

Then sew back along the spine in the opposite direction. Tie the two loose ends together.

# MAKING COVERS

The simplest kind of cover to make is a soft card wrapper. However, if you want the book to be really strong and long-lasting, you could try gluing the pages into a hard cover, with a spine made from cotton tape or bias binding.

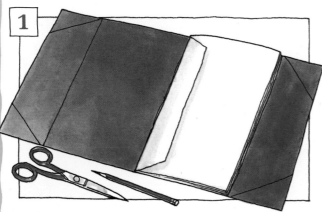

## Wrapper Cover

Measure and cut out a piece of thick paper, the same height as the pages of your book, but twice as wide, and with a wide flap at either end.

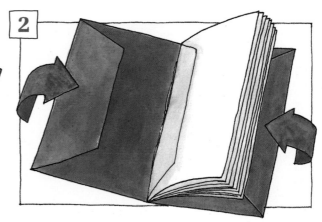

Trim the wrapper flaps top and bottom, then score and fold them in. Fold the wrapper in half, and lay the book inside.

Cut a flap in the middle of the front and back pages. Fold and tuck in the cover flaps, as shown.

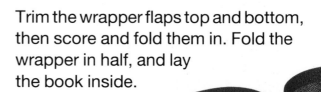

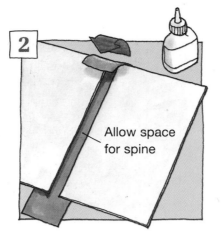

Allow space for spine

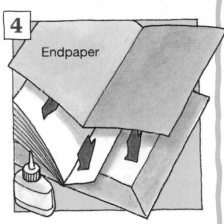

## Hard Cover

Cut out two pieces of strong card. Make them about 4 mm wider than the pages of your book on all sides.

Glue the pieces onto a strip of cloth, allowing an extra 4 cm at the top and bottom. Fold the extra bits over, and glue.

Cut two pieces of paper, 5 cm wider than the boards on the top, outer and bottom edges. Then trim the corners of the papers, and glue to the boards as shown.

Endpaper

Glue the back of the piece of strengthening card to the cover. Then glue the first and last pages of the book to the inside of the covers. Or, you could cut two separate endpapers from coloured paper, and glue them between the cover and the book.

# PRINTING PATTERNS

Try printing designs onto your covers – use poster paints for the stencils and printing blocks, and oil paints for marbling.

You can also make beautiful patterned endpapers in the same way, or even print directly onto the pages of your book.

# Stencilling

Draw a design onto stencilling card, or ordinary thin card. Carefully cut out the holes with a craft knife.

Hold the card down on the cover, and dab thick poster paint over the holes with a piece of sponge, or a stencilling brush.

# Printing Blocks

Cut some shapes out of foam rubber, and glue them to thick squares of wood or card.

Dip the shapes into thick paint, and press them down to print. When the paint is dry, you could add some extra details, using a darker colour.

# Marbling

Half-fill a wide tray with water. Mix some oil paints with white spirit until runny, then dribble them across the water.

Swirl the water gently with a clean brush, then lay a sheet of paper on top.

Smooth gently, lift off, and leave to dry.

# COLLAGE COVERS

Magazines, newspapers and greetings cards can all be cut up and glued to your covers to make a collage. You can also use bits of old junk to make pictures and patterns – these look best if you paint them afterwards. A coat of polyurethane varnish will stop the paint from rubbing off the covers.

### Collage Castle

This castle was made from tree bark, kitchen foil, sandpaper, some cocktail sticks, pencils and bamboo – but you could use all kinds of spare junk! The moon was made from half a cashew nut.

The castle was then painted silvery-grey once the glue was dry.

### Découpage

Cut pictures out of old wrapping paper, magazines or newspapers, and glue them to your cover to make an overlapping pattern.

Look for interesting colours, pictures and shades. Try tearing some of the pages – this gives a softer edge than cutting them.

### Antique Book

Cut out some shapes from card, and some short lengths of string. Glue them to the cover in a pattern.

Brush black paint along the raised edges, then leave to dry. Rub gold paint over the cover with a dry brush.

# BOOKMARKS

Make bookmarks from spare bits of card! If your book has a theme, your bookmark could match it – for example, a monster bookmark could hang over the pages of a scary story!

**1** Draw and cut out a bookmark from card. Paint it, or decorate it by gluing on some shapes cut from card. Draw a flap, and cut it out with a craft knife.

**2** Slot the flap over one of the pages in your book. You could also make a flap by gluing on an extra piece of card (like the parrot's wing, see right) – only the top should be glued to the bookmark.

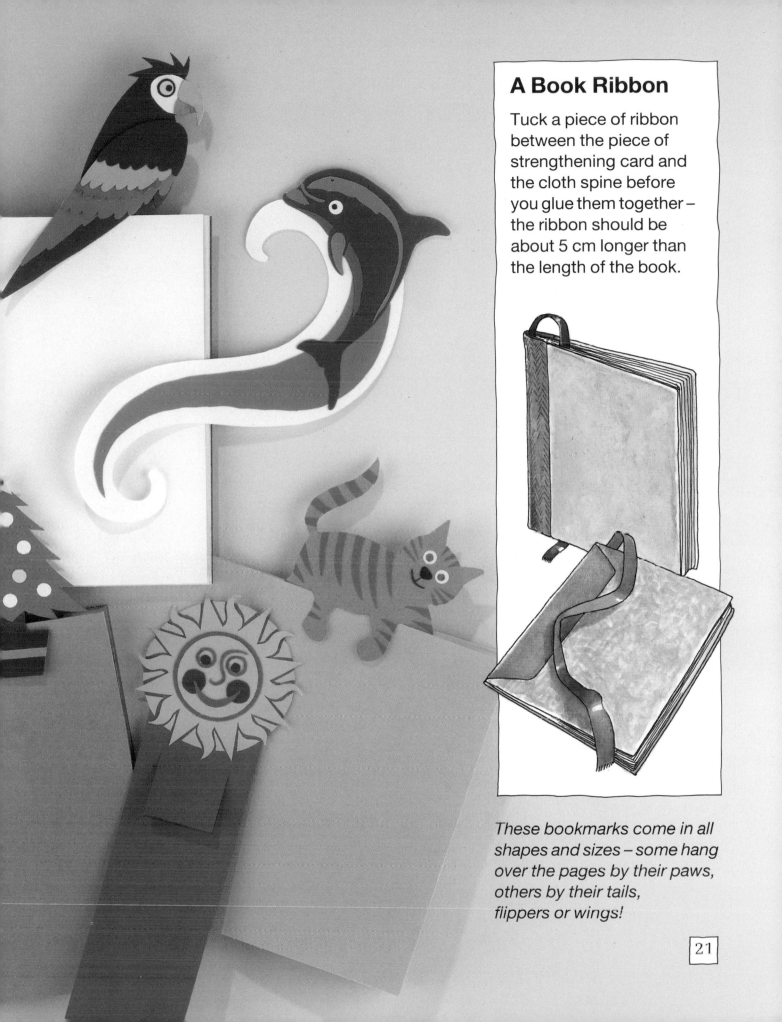

## A Book Ribbon

Tuck a piece of ribbon between the piece of strengthening card and the cloth spine before you glue them together – the ribbon should be about 5 cm longer than the length of the book.

*These bookmarks come in all shapes and sizes – some hang over the pages by their paws, others by their tails, flippers or wings!*

# DESIGNING BOOKS

Now you've made your book, what are you going to do with it? You may want to use the book as a diary or a notebook, or to give it to someone as a gift. On the other hand, you could use it to write and illustrate a story, a poem, or anything else at all. Here's how you go about it.

Count how many pages you have in your book, then draw them on a piece of paper. This is called a *page plan*. It will help you to work out where you want your text and illustrations to go.

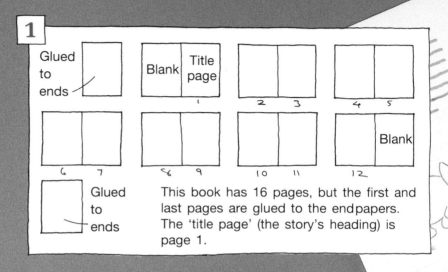

**1**

Glued to ends

Blank | Title page

1    2   3    4   5

6   7    8   9    10   11    12

Blank

Glued to ends

This book has 16 pages, but the first and last pages are glued to the endpapers. The 'title page' (the story's heading) is page 1.

**2**

Decide how many lines of text to put on each page. Some pages can have more text than others, as you can see from the designs shown in the photo.

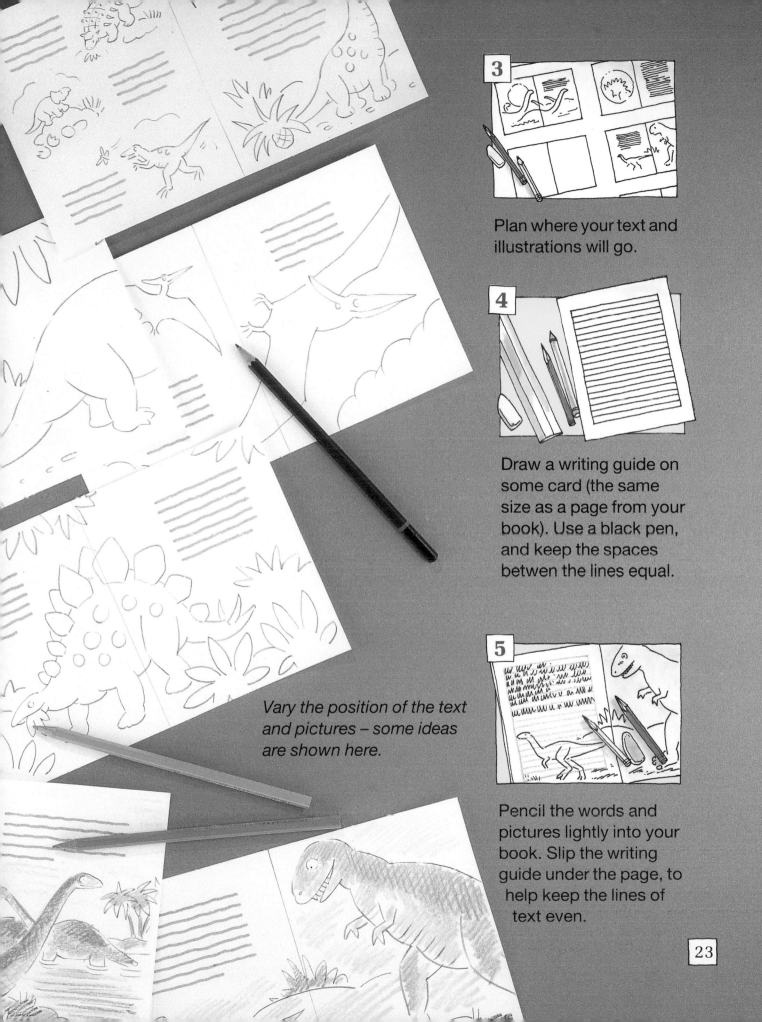

**3**

Plan where your text and illustrations will go.

**4**

Draw a writing guide on some card (the same size as a page from your book). Use a black pen, and keep the spaces betwen the lines equal.

*Vary the position of the text and pictures – some ideas are shown here.*

**5**

Pencil the words and pictures lightly into your book. Slip the writing guide under the page, to help keep the lines of text even.

# ADDING PICTURES

When you're happy with the way your designs are looking, you can take your pens and paints and fill in the words and pictures.

Do the illustrations first, using some of the suggestions on these pages. Then carefully write the words around the pictures.

*The dinosaur spreads below were painted, while the planets and rockets were made by sticking down pieces of card and paper.*

*The spread on the far right shows how magazines can be cut up and arranged to make fun collage pictures.*

## Painting

You can draw or paint the illustrations directly onto the pages. Or trace some pictures from your favourite books and magazines, and colour them in.

## Paper Shapes

Cut shapes out of card, or paper, and glue them to the pages to make pictures (most of the photos in this book show books that have been illustrated in this way).

## Collage

Cut pictures from old colour magazines, and glue them into your book.

You could also use newspapers, photos you've taken yourself, or photocopies.

# NOVELTY NOTEBOOKS

Notebooks can be quickly sewn or stapled to make presents for birthdays or Christmas — they can be any shape or size, as long as you remember to leave most of the folded edge uncut. You can either leave the insides blank, or write in special messages or information.

**1**

Fold several sheets of thick paper together. Draw on the design for your book, and sew down the middle of the pages (see page 11).

**2**

Cut around the outline of the notebook, as shown. Make sure you don't cut any of the thread that holds the spine of the book together.

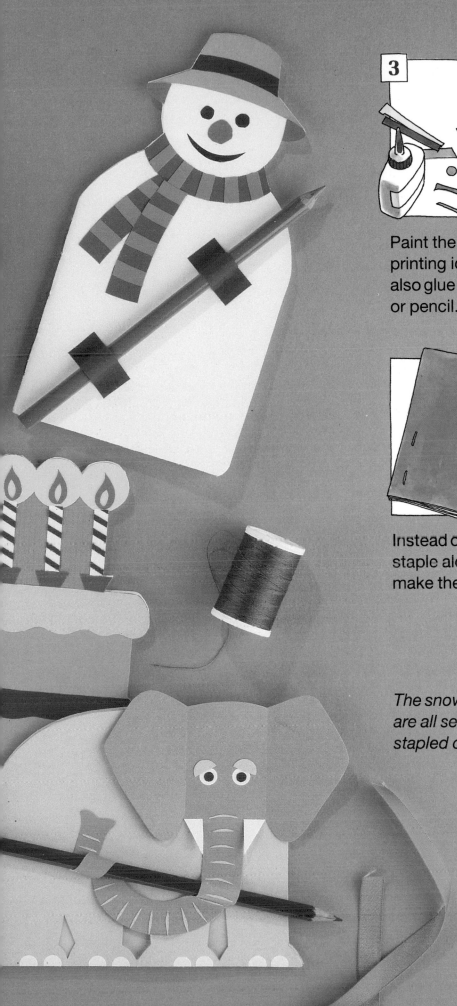

Paint the front, or use some of the printing ideas on page 17. You could also glue on loops of card, to hold a pen or pencil.

Instead of sewing the books, you could staple along the spine – as we did to make the birthday cake book.

*The snowman, elephant and sunflower are all sewn. The birthday cake book is stapled down the side.*

*To make the butterfly, cut several wing-shaped pages, and sew down the middle. Cut out the body separately, and glue it over the stitches.*

# ZIG-ZAG BOOKS

Zig-zag books don't need any sewing! They can be written and read just like ordinary books, or unfolded and pinned to the wall to make a frieze.

These books look best if you make them out of stiff paper, or thin card.

**1**

## Simple Zig-zag

Divide a long strip of thin card or thick paper into equal parts, using a ruler and a pencil.

Fold the paper up into a zig-zag. Then add your illustrations and text (if any).

**2**

Decorate both sides – use them to make long, fold-out friezes, or to tell a story.

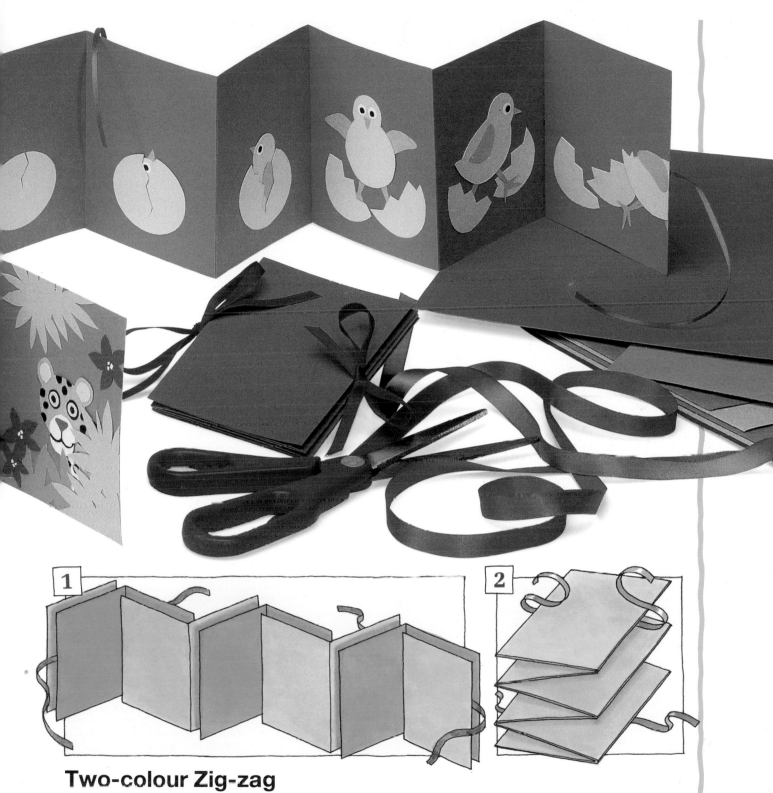

## Two-colour Zig-zag

Take three sheets of paper in one colour, and three in another colour. Fold them in half, and cut one of the pieces in two. Glue together to make a zig-zag, with the two cut pieces at each end.

You could glue some ribbon under the end pieces, as shown, to tie up the zig-zag.

# POP-UP BOOKS

How about having pop-up pictures in your books? They look very impressive, but aren't that difficult to make. Like the flaps and moving parts on pages 33-36, pop-ups work best in books of less than ten pages, using thin card rather than paper.

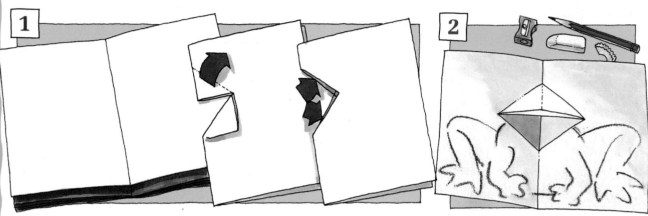

**1**

**2**

## Mouths and Beaks

Cut a piece of card, the same size as a spread in your book. Fold the paper, and cut a slit near the middle. Fold back the flaps, and tuck in.

When you open the page, the flaps will open like a mouth or beak!

**3**

Colour in the picture, then glue the page into your book. Don't put any glue on the back of the mouth or beak.

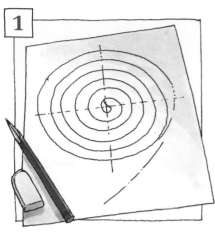

**1**

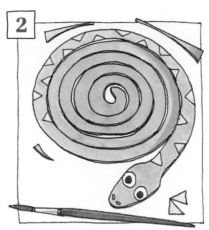

**2**

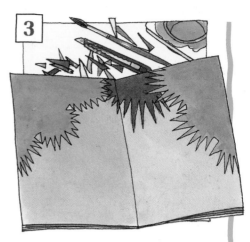

**3**

## Spirals

Draw a circle on a piece of thin card, slightly smaller than a page from your book. Draw a spiral inside the circle.

Draw a snake's head at the outer edge of the circle, as shown. Cut around all the lines with scissors.

Use paints, felt-tips or bits of coloured paper to decorate the snake, and to make a colourful jungle background.

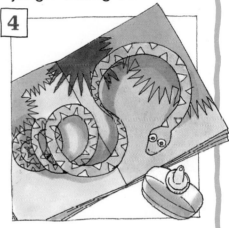

**4**

Glue the *back* of the snake's head to the right-hand page. Put a blob of glue on the *top* of its tail. Shut the book, press together, then open and leave to dry.

*You can glue on extra details made from card, such as this frog's bulging eyes!*

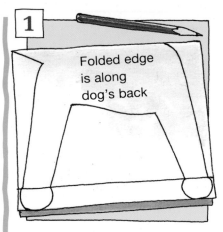 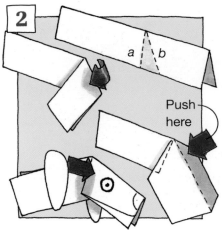 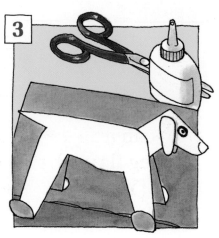

## Stand-up Dog

Fold a 14 x 8 cm piece of card in half. Draw the shape of the dog's body as shown, and cut it out so that the folded edge is along the dog's back.

Fold a 9 x 4 cm piece of card in half. Make the folds *a* and *b*, then open and push downwards to make the head. Cut and glue on the ears.

Glue the neck into the body. Fold back the paws on one side, and glue the undersides to one of the pages, 1.5 cm from the gutter.

Fold back the paws on the other side. Dab the undersides with glue, and fold the facing page on top of them.

*You can decorate your stand-up animals before gluing them into your book. This dog's spots were made with a hole-puncher, and then glued to the body.*

# FLAPS & MOVERS

You can add even more fun and excitement to your books by making flaps that open, holes to peep through, and wheels that turn! (You could also use these methods to make really special greetings cards.)

## Flaps

Simple doors and windows can be glued directly into your book.

You can also cut out flaps from a separate page of card, and glue the page into the book.

## Peepholes

Peepholes such as keyholes and window panes can be cut from the cover or inside pages, to show part of the picture on the page underneath.

## Mix and Match

Cut a small book into three sections. Draw a figure on the front. Open the flaps, and mark where the neck and legs join. Draw a new figure on each page.

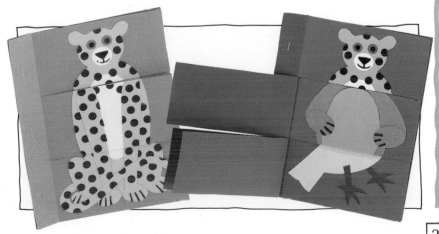

**1**

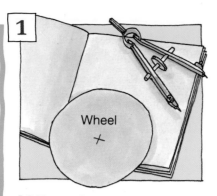

## Wheels

Cut out a card wheel,
1 cm smaller than a page
in your book.

**2**

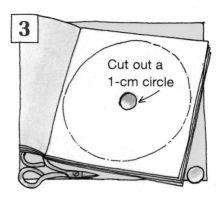

Put the wheel on the
page, and draw around
it. Mark both centres.

**3**

Measure a 1-cm circle
around the mark on the
page, and cut it out.

**4**

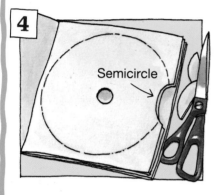

Cut a semicircle from the
page edge, and also
from the page beneath it.

**5**

Cut out a window,
leaving 1 cm between
the outer edge of the

circle and the window,
and 1 cm between the
window and the centre.

**6**

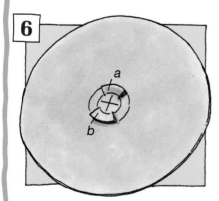

Draw a 2-cm circle in the
middle of the wheel, with
a 1-cm circle inside it.
Cut and fold up flaps *a*
and *b* as shown.

**7**

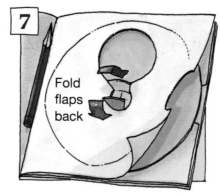

Lay the wheel under the
page, and push the flaps
through the hole. Turn
the wheel round, and
draw inside the window.

**8**

Glue the edges of the
page to the one under-
neath. Then glue another
small circle to the flaps –
*not* to the page.

Your wheel could show ghosts
in a haunted castle . . . or a
changing view from a porthole!

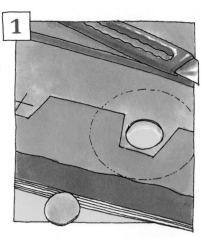

**1**

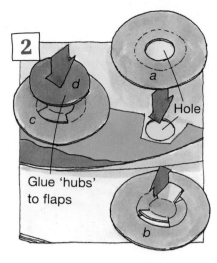

**2**

a

Hole

c  d

Glue 'hubs'
to flaps

b

**3**

# Moving Machines

Draw a machine onto a page in your book, or make the picture from shapes cut from card. Draw the outline of a wheel, and cut a 1-cm circle from the middle of the wheel.

Cut two card wheels, one with flaps (see page 34), and one with a 1-cm hole in the centre. Assemble the wheel as shown. Then cut a 'hub' from card, and glue it onto the flaps.

You can join other moving parts in the same way. Just cut a hole in one of the parts, and flaps in the other. Slot together as shown, and cover with circles cut from card.

# PEEP-IN BOOKS

Here's a very special book-making project, and once again, it's much simpler than it looks! The book has five spreads, so if you want to use it for a story or a poem, you'll have to divide your text into five separate sections.

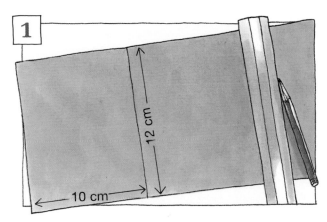

**1**

To make the background for the book, cut a long strip of card measuring 12 x 100 cm. Use a ruler to divide it into ten 10-cm-wide pages, as shown.

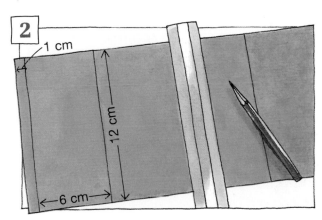

**2**

Cut a strip measuring 12 x 62 cm for the foreground. Allow a 1-cm flap at each end, and divide the rest of the strip into ten 6-cm-wide pages.

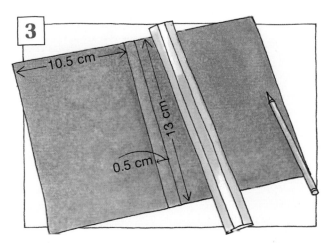

**3**

Cut a slightly thicker piece of card for the cover (21.5 x 13 cm). Measure a 0.5-cm-wide spine down the middle, and score along the lines.

**4**

Draw and colour up the five background spreads (each spread is made up of two pages). It's best to keep these pictures quite simple.

You can use paints to decorate the foreground and background, or glue down shapes cut from card, as here.

**5**

Draw your illustrations onto the five foreground spreads. Cut peepholes in each one. Paint the spreads, or glue down cut-out pictures.

**6**

Fold both the strips carefully into zig-zags, as shown above. Fold the two 1-cm flaps at both ends of the foreground strip outwards.

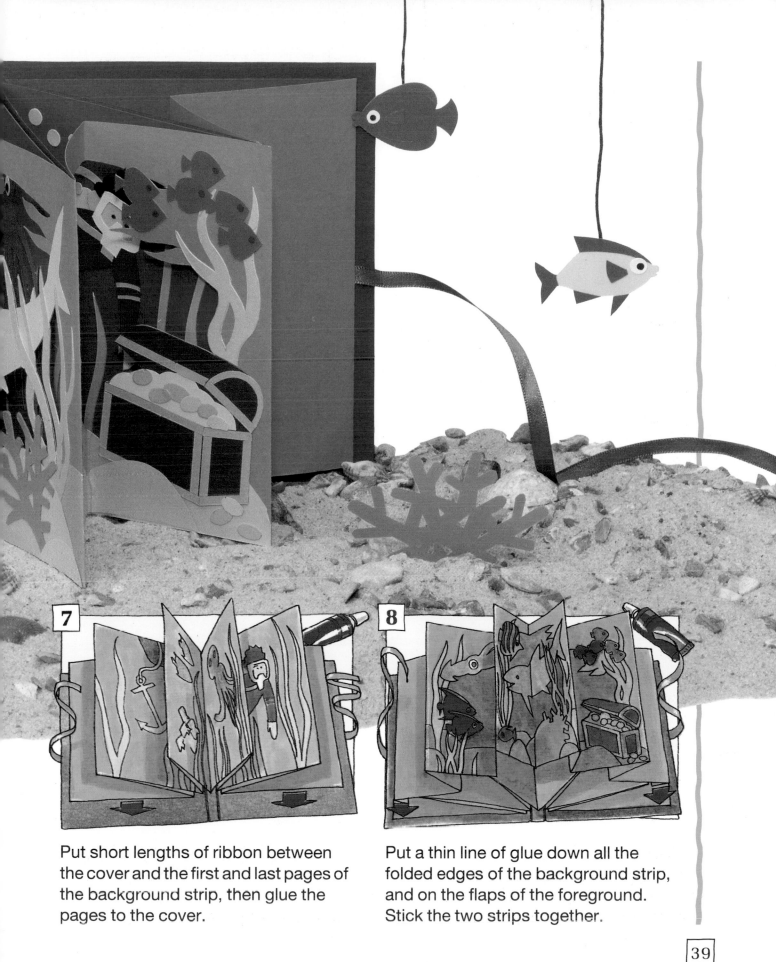

**7** Put short lengths of ribbon between the cover and the first and last pages of the background strip, then glue the pages to the cover.

**8** Put a thin line of glue down all the folded edges of the background strip, and on the flaps of the foreground. Stick the two strips together.

Several books can be put into a box called a *slipcase*. Cut the case shape shown from card, using the size of the books as a guide.

The length and width of the case should be about 1 cm longer than the books, and the depth should be 1 cm wider than the spines of the books when they're stacked together. Add flaps, then fold up and glue into a case.

Length

Width

Depth

Flap

Slipcase

Fridge magnet notebook

Scroll

Scrolls were among the earliest types of book. Make one by rolling up a sheet of paper, and tying with ribbon – add a 'seal' cut from card, if you like.

Try gluing a magnet to the back of a tiny book, and fixing it to the fridge!